JOY TO THE WORLD

Daily Readings For Advent

Charles H. Spurgeon

Spurgeon Daily Substack

For daily encouragement from Spurgeon's archives, try spurgeondaily.substack.com

Contents

Introduction

In the midst of the business of December, take 5 minutes each day and let Spurgeon warm your heart with joy that can only be found in the good news of Jesus Christ.

"This is the season of the year when, whether we wish it or not, we are compelled to think of the birth of Christ." said Charles Spurgeon at the start of his sermon on 23rd December 1855. After dispelling any notion of a religious necessity of celebrating Christmas, he went on, "However, I wish there were ten or a dozen Christmas-days in the year" as an opportunity to preach on the incarnation of Jesus.

Slow down this advent and reflect on the birth of Jesus

Recommended reading:

The Bank of Faith: 365 daily devotional readings from Charles Spurgeon

All Things New: Daily devotional readings for January from Charles Spurgeon

The Cross: 40 daily devotional readings on the cross of Christ from Charles Spurgeon

A Child is Born: daily readings for advent from Charles Spurgeon

Day 1 - The First Act Of Grace

*"I will put enmity between you and the woman,
and between your offspring and her offspring;
he shall bruise your head, and you shall bruise
his heel."*
(Genesis 3:15 ESV)

This is the first gospel sermon that was ever delivered upon the surface of this earth. It was memorable discourse indeed, with Jehovah himself for the preacher, and the whole human race and the prince of darkness for the audience. It must be worthy of our heartiest attention.

Is it not remarkable that this great gospel promise should have been delivered so soon after the transgression? As yet, no sentence had been pronounced upon either of the two human offenders, but the promise was given under the form of a sentence pronounced upon the serpent.

Not yet had the woman been condemned to painful travail, or the man to exhausting labour, or even the soil to the curse of thorn and thistle. Before the Lord had said "you are dust and to dust you shall return[1]" he was pleased to say that the seed of the woman should bruise the serpent's head. Let us rejoice, then, in the swift mercy of God, which in the early watches of the night of sin came with comfortable words unto us.

We do not know what our first parents understood by it, but we may be certain that they gathered a great amount of comfort from it. They must have understood that they were not then and there to be destroyed, because the Lord had spoken of a "seed." They would argue that it must be needful that Eve should live if there should be a seed from her. They understood, too, that if that seed was to overcome the serpent and bruise his head, it must predict good for themselves. They could not fail to see that there was some great, mysterious benefit to be conferred upon them by the victory which their seed would achieve over the instigator of their ruin.

---

[1] Genesis 3:19

That seed of the woman that glorious One - for he speaks not of *seeds* as in many but of *seed* as is one - you know how he abhorred the devil and all his devices. There was enmity between Christ and Satan, for he came to destroy the works of the devil and to deliver those who are under bondage to him. For that purpose was he born; for that purpose did he live; for that purpose did he die; for that purpose he has gone into the glory, and for that purpose he will come again - that everywhere he may find out his adversary and utterly destroy him and his works from amongst the sons of men. This putting of the enmity between the two seeds was the commencement of the plan of mercy, the first act in the programme of grace.[2]

---

[2] Christ the Conqueror of Satan - Sermon delivered November 26th 1876

Day 2 - A Swinging Blow For The Devil

"I will put enmity between you and the woman, and between your offspring and her offspring; he shall bruise your head, and you shall bruise his heel."
(Genesis 3:15 ESV)

Christ [would be] bruised by the old serpent. That is all, however! It is only his heel, not his head, which is bruised! For lo, the Champion rises again; the bruise was not mortal nor continual. Though he dies, so brief is the interval in which he slumbers in the tomb that his holy body hath not seen corruption, and he comes forth perfect and lovely in his manhood, rising from his grave as from a refreshing sleep after so long a day of unresting toil!

By his sufferings Christ has overthrown Satan, by the heel that was bruised he has trodden upon the head which devised the bruising.

He comes to us in mercy, and puts enmity between us and the serpent. That is the very first work of grace. There was peace between us and Satan once; when he tempted we yielded; whatever he taught us we believed; we were his willing slaves. But perhaps you can recollect when first of all you began to feel uneasy and dissatisfied; the world's pleasures no longer pleased you; all the juice seemed to have been taken out of the apple, and you had nothing at all. Then you suddenly perceived that you were living in sin, and you were miserable about it, and though you could not get rid of sin you hated it, and sighed over it, and cried, and groaned. In your heart of hearts you remained no longer on the side of evil, for you began to cry, "O wretched man that I am, who shall deliver me from the body of this death?"[3] You were already, in the covenant of grace, ordained to be the woman's seed, and now the decree began to discover itself in life bestowed upon you and working in you. The Lord in infinite mercy dropped the divine life into your soul. You did not know it, but there it was, a spark of the celestial fire, the living and incorruptible seed which abideth for ever.

---

[3] Romans 7:24

The great power of the serpent lies in unpardoned sin. He cries "I have made you guilty: I brought you under the curse." 'No," say we, "we are delivered from the curse and are now blessed, for it is written, 'Blessed is the man whose transgression is forgiven, whose sin is covered.'[4] We are no longer guilty, for who shall lay anything to the charge of God's elect?[5] Since Christ has justified, who is he that condemns?

This is a swinging blow for the old dragon's head, from which he will never recover.[6]

---

[4] Psalm 32:1, Romans 4:7

[5] Romans 8:33

[6] Christ the Conqueror of Satan - Sermon delivered November 26th 1876

Day 3 - House Of Bread Or War

But you, O Bethlehem Ephrathah, who are too little to be among the clans of Judah, from you shall come forth for me one who is to be ruler in Israel, whose coming forth is from of old, from ancient days.
(Micah 5:2 ESV)

The word Bethlehem has a double meaning. It signifies "the house of bread," and "the house of war."

Ought not Jesus Christ to be born in "the house of bread?" He is the Bread of his people, on which they feed. As our fathers ate manna in the wilderness, so do we live on Jesus here below. Famished by the world, we cannot feed on its shadows. Its husks may gratify the swinish taste of worldlings, for they are swine; but we need something more substantial, and in that blest bread of heaven, made of the bruised body of our Lord Jesus, and baked in the furnace of his agonies, we find a blessed food.

There is no food like Jesus to the desponding soul or to the strongest saint. The very meanest of the family of God goes to Bethlehem for his bread; and the strongest man, who eats strong meat, goes to Bethlehem for it. House of Bread! Where else could our nourishment come from but from you?

[Bethlehem] is also called "the house of war;" because Christ is to a man "the house of bread," or else "the house of war." While he is food to the righteous, he causes war to the wicked, according to his own word - "Think not that I am come to send peace on the earth; I am not come to send peace, but a sword. For I am come to set a man at variance against his father, and the daughter against her mother, and the daughter-in-law against her mother-in-law. And a man's foes shall be they of his own household."[7]

If you do not know Bethlehem as "the house of bread," it shall be to you a "house of war." If from the lips of Jesus you never drink sweet honey, then out of the same mouth there shall

---

[7] Matthew 10:34-35

go forth against you a two-edged sword; and that mouth from which the righteous draw their bread, shall be to you the mouth of destruction. Jesus of Bethlehem, house of bread and house of war, we trust we know you as our bread. Oh! that some who are now at war with you might hear in their hearts, as well as in their ears the song -

"Peace on earth, and mercy mild.

God and sinners reconciled."[8]

And now for that word Ephratah That was the old name of the place which the Jews retained and loved. The meaning of it is, "fruitfulness," or "abundance." Ah! Where does my fruitfulness come from but from Bethlehem? Our poor barren hearts never produced one fruit, or flower, till they were watered with the Saviour blood. It is his incarnation which fattens the soil of our hearts. There had been pricking thorns on all the ground, and mortal poisons, before he came; but our fruitfulness comes from him.[9]

---

[8] Hark the Herald Angels Sing

[9] The Incarnation and Birth of Christ - Sermon delivered 23rd December 1855

Day 4 - Born A King

But you, O Bethlehem Ephrathah, who are too little to be among the clans of Judah, from you shall come forth for me one who is to be ruler in Israel, whose coming forth is from of old, from ancient days.
(Micah 5:2 ESV)

Bethlehem is said to be "little among the clans of Judah." Why is this? Because Jesus Christ always goes among little ones. He was born in the little one "among the clans of Judah." No Bashan's high hill, not on Hebron's royal mount, not in Jerusalem's palaces. but the humble, yet illustrious, village of Bethlehem. There are some little ones among you - "little among the clans of Judah." No one ever heard your name, did they? If you were buried, and had your name on your tombstone, it would never be noticed. Those who pass by would say, "it is nothing to me: I never knew him." You do not know much of yourself, or think much of yourself. You are despised amongst men; or, if you are not despised by them, you despise yourself. You are one of the little ones. Well, Christ is born in Bethlehem among the little ones. Big hearts never get Christ inside of them; Christ lies not in great hearts, but in little ones. Mighty and proud spirits never have Jesus Christ, for he comes in at low doors, but he will not come in at high ones. He who has a broken heart, and a low spirit, shall have the Saviour, but no one else.

A very unique thing is this - that Jesus Christ was said to have been "born the king of the Jews." Very few have ever been "born king." Men are born princes, but they are seldom born kings. I do not think you can find an instance in history where any infant was born king. He was the prince of Wales, perhaps, and he had to wait a number of years, till his father died, and then they manufactured him into a king, by putting a crown on his head; but he was not born a king. I remember no one who was born a king except Jesus. ; and there is emphatic meaning in that verse that we sing:

"Born thy people to deliver;

Born a child, and yet a king."[10]

The moment that he came on earth he was a king.[11]

---

[10] Come, thou long expected Jesus

[11] The Incarnation and Birth of Christ - Sermon delivered 23rd December 1855

Day 5 - Everlasting Love

*But you, O Bethlehem Ephrathah, who are too little to be among the clans of Judah, from you shall come forth for me one who is to be ruler in Israel, **whose coming forth is from of old, from ancient days**.*
(Micah 5:2 ESV)

Not only when you were born into the world did Christ love you, but his delights were with the sons of men before there were any sons of men. Often did he think of them; from everlasting to everlasting he had set his affection upon them. Believer, has he been so long about your salvation, will he not accomplish it? Has he from everlasting been going forth to save me, and will he lose me now? Has he had me in his hand, as his precious jewel, and will he now let me slip between his precious fingers? Did he choose me before the mountains were brought forth, or the channels of the deep scooped out, and will he lose me now? Impossible!

I am sure he would not love me so long, and then leave off loving me. If he intended to be tired of me, he would have been tired of me long before now. If he had not loved me with a love as deep as hell and as unutterable as the grave, if he had not given his whole heart to me, I am sure he would have turned from me long ago. He knew what I would be, and he has had long time enough to consider of it; but I am his choice. He is contented with me - he must be contented with me, for he has known me long enough to know my faults. He knew me before I knew myself; he knew me before I was myself. Long before my members were fashioned they were written in his book, his eyes of affection were set on them. He knew how badly I would act towards him, and yet he has continued to love me.[12]

---

[12] The Incarnation and Birth of Christ - Sermon delivered 23rd December 1855

Day 6 - Invisible Strings

In those days a decree went out from Caesar Augustus that all the world should be registered. This was the first registration when Quirinius was governor of Syria. And all went to be registered, each to his own town. And Joseph also went up from Galilee, from the town of Nazareth, to Judea, to the city of David, which is called Bethlehem, because he was of the house and lineage of David, to be registered with Mary, his betrothed, who was with child.
(Luke 2:1-5 ESV)

[It had been prophesied] that our Lord [would spring] out of Judah. It was necessary, also, that he should be born in Bethlehem, according to the word of the Lord which he spoke by his servant Micah.[13] But how could a public recognition of the lineage of an obscure carpenter and an unknown maiden be procured? What interest could the keepers of registers be supposed to take in two such humble persons? As for the second matter, Mary lived at Nazareth in Galilee, and there

---

[13] Micah 2:7

seemed every probability that the birth would take place there; indeed, the period of her delivery was so near that, unless absolutely compelled, she would not be likely to undertake a long and tedious journey to the southern province of Judea. How are these two matters to be arranged?

A little tyrant, Herod, by some show of independent spirit, offends the greater tyrant, Augustus. Augustus informs him that he shall no longer treat him as a friend, but as a vassal. Although Herod makes the most abject submission, and his friends at the Roman court intercede for him, Augustus, to show his displeasure, orders a census to be taken of all the Jewish people, in readiness for taxation, which, however, was not carried out till some ten years after. Even the winds and waves are not more fickle than a tyrant's will; but the Ruler of tempests knows how to rule the perverse spirits of princes. The Lord our God has a bit for the wildest war horse, and a hook for the most terrible leviathan. Autocratical Caesars are but puppets moved with invisible strings, mere drudges to the King of kings.[14]

[14] No room for Christ in the inn - Sermon delivered December 21st 1862

Day 7 - Laid In A Manger

And she gave birth to her firstborn son and wrapped him in swaddling cloths and laid him in a manger, because there was no place for them in the inn.
(Luke 2:7 ESV)

The manger and the cross standing at the two extremities of the Savior's earthly life seem most fit and congruous to each other. He is to wear, through life, a peasant's garb; he is to associate with fishermen; the lowly are to be his disciples; the cold mountains are often to be his only bed; he is to say, "Foxes have holes, and the birds of the air have nests, but the Son of Man has nowhere to lay his head"[15]

Nothing, therefore, could be more fitting than that in his season of humiliation, when he laid aside all his glory, and took upon himself the form of a servant, and condescended even to the meanest estate, he should be laid in a manger.

---

[15] Luke 9:58

The King of Men who was born in Bethlehem, was not exempted in his infancy from the common calamities of the poor. No, his lot was even worse than theirs. I think I hear the shepherds comment on the manger-birth, "Ah!" said one to his fellow, "then he will not be like Herod the tyrant; he will remember the manger and feel for the poor; poor helpless infant, I feel a love for him even now, what miserable accommodation this cold world yields its Savior. It is not a Caesar that is born to-day; he will never trample down our fields with his armies, or slaughter our flocks for his courtiers, he will be the poor man's friend, the people's monarch. According to the words of our shepherd-king, he shall judge the poor of the people; he shall save the children of the needy." Surely the shepherds, and those like them - the poor of the earth - perceived at once that here was the plebeian king; noble in descent, but still as the Lord called him, "one chosen out of the people."[16]

Great Prince of Peace! The manger was your royal cradle! There you were presented to all nations as Prince of our race, before whose

---

[16] Psalm 89:19

presence there is neither barbarian, Scythian, bond nor free; but you are Lord of all. Kings, your gold and silver would have been lavished on him if you had known the Lord of Glory. The things which are not, under him shall bring to nothing the things that are, and the things that are despised which God has chosen, shall under his leadership break in pieces the might, and pride, and majesty of human grandeur.[17]

---

[17] No room for Christ in the inn - Sermon delivered December 21st 1862

Day 8 - Do Not Shut Yourself Out

And she gave birth to her firstborn son and wrapped him in swaddling cloths and laid him in a manger, because there was no place for them in the inn.
(Luke 2:7 ESV)

In being laid in a manger, he did, as it were, give an invitation to the most humble to come to him. We might tremble to approach a throne, but we cannot fear to approach a manger.

Never could there be a being more approachable than Christ.

Our Lord Jesus Christ was born in the stable of the inn to show how free he is to all comers. The Gospel is preached to every creature and shuts out none. We may say of the invitations of Holy Scripture:

"None are excluded hence but those

Who do themselves exclude;

Welcome the learned and polite,

The ignorant and rude.

Though Jesus' grace can save the prince,

The poor may take their share;

No mortal has a just pretense

To perish in despairs."

If you desire to come to Christ you may come to him just as you are; you may come now. Whoever has the desire in his heart to trust Christ is free to do it. Jesus is free to you; he will receive you; he will welcome you with gladness, and to show this, I think, the young child was cradled in a manger. We know that sinners often imagine that they are shut out. Often, the convicted conscience will write bitter things against itself and deny its part in mercy's stores.

Brothers and sisters, if God has not shut you out, do not shut yourself out.[18]

---

[18] No room for Christ in the inn - Sermon delivered December 21st 1862

Day 9 - No Room In Religion

And she gave birth to her firstborn son and
wrapped him in swaddling cloths and laid him in
a manger, because there was no place for them
in the inn.
(Luke 2:7 ESV)

[Is there] some room for Christ in what is called good society? Were there not in Bethlehem some people that were very respectable, who kept themselves aloof from the common multitude; people of reputation and standing - could not they find room for Christ? Dear friends, there is no room for Him in what is called good society. There is room for all the silly little forms by which men choose to restrict themselves; room for the vain niceties of etiquette; room for frivolous conversation; room for the adoration of the body, there is room for the setting up of this and that as the idol of the hour. But there is too little room for Christ, and it is far from fashionable to follow the Lord fully.

Should you begin to talk about the things of Christ in many a circle, you would be tabooed at once. "I will never ask that man to my house again," so-and-so would say - "if he must bring his religion with him." Folly and finery, rank and honor, jewels and glitter, frivolity and fashion, all report that there is no room for Jesus in their abodes. There is a public opinion upon every subject; and you know there is tolerance in this country to everything but Christ.

The most accursed enemies of true religion have been the men who pretended to be its advocates. The false hirelings that are not Christ's shepherds, and love not his sheep, have ever been the most ferocious enemies of our God and of his Christ. There is no room for him where his name is chanted in solemn hymns and his image lifted up amid smoke of incense. Go anywhere, and there is no space for the Prince of peace other than with the humble and contrite spirits which by grace he prepares to give him shelter.

I would give not a farthing for your religion, nay, not even the turn of a rusty nail. If God's Word be true, every atom of it, then we should act upon it.[19]

---

[19] No room for Christ in the inn - Sermon delivered December 21st 1862

Day 10 - Have You Room?

And she gave birth to her firstborn son and wrapped him in swaddling cloths and laid him in a manger, because there was no place for them in the inn.
(Luke 2:7 ESV)

How little room is there for Christ in general conversation. We talk about many things, speech is very free in this land; but, ah! how little room is there for Christ in general talk! Even on Sunday afternoon how little room there is for Christ in some professed Christian's houses. They will talk about ministers, tell anecdotes about them; they will talk about the Sunday school, or the various agencies in connection with the Church, but how little they say about Christ! And if some one should in conversation make this remark, "Could we not speak upon the Godhead and manhood, the finished work and righteousness, the ascension, or the second advent of our Lord Jesus Christ," why we should see many, who even profess to be followers of Christ, who would hold up their heads and say, "Why, dear, that man is quite a fanatic, or else he would not think of introducing such a subject as that into general conversation." No, there is no room for him in the inn.

The palace, the forum, and the inn have no room for Christ. Have you room for Christ?

"Well," says one, "I have room for him, but I am not worthy that he should come to me." Ah! I did not ask about worthiness; have you room for him? "Oh," says one, "I have an empty void the world can never fill!" Ah! I see you have room for him. "Oh! but the room I have in my heart is so base!" So was the manger. "But it is so despicable!" So was the manger a thing to be despised. "Ah! but my heart is so foul!" So, perhaps, the manger may have been. "Oh! but I feel it is a place not at all fit for Christ!" Nor was the manger a place fit for him, and yet there was he laid." Oh! but I have been such a sinner; I feel as if my heart had been a den of beasts and devils!" Well, the manger had been a place where beasts had fed. Have you room for him? Never mind what the past has been; he can forget and forgive.

Oh! I have such a free Christ to preach! I have such a precious loving, Jesus to preach, he is willing to find a home in humble hearts.[20]

---

[20]   No room for Christ in the inn - Sermon delivered December 21st 1862

Day 11 - The Greatest Possible Joy

And the angel said to them, "Fear not, for behold, I bring you good news of great joy that will be for all the people.
(Luke 2:10 ESV)

In our text we have before us the sermon of the first evangelist of the gospel. The preacher was an angel, and the key-note of this angelic gospel is joy—"I bring you good news of great joy."

Nature fears in the presence of God—the shepherds were afraid. The law itself served to deepen this natural feeling of dismay. People were sinful, and the law came into the world to reveal sin, its tendency was to make men fear and tremble under any and every divine revelation. The Jews unanimously believed that if any man saw supernatural appearances, he would be sure to die. But the first word of the gospel ended all this, for the angelic evangelist said, "Fear not, behold I bring you good news."

Henceforth, it is no longer a dreadful thing for man to approach his Maker. Redeemed man is not to fear when God unveils the splendor of his majesty, since he appears no more a judge upon his throne of terror, but a Father unbending in sacred familiarity before his own beloved children.

The joy which this first gospel preacher spoke of was no little joy, for [the news was] not good news of joy only, but "good news of great joy." Every word is emphatic, as if to show that the gospel is, above all things, intended to promote, and will abundantly create the greatest possible joy in the human heart wherever it is received. Man is like a harp unstrung, and the music of his soul's living strings is discordant, his whole nature wails with sorrow; but the son of David, that mighty harpist, has come to restore the harmony of humanity, and where his gracious fingers move among the strings, the touch of the fingers of an incarnate God brings forth music sweet as that of the spheres, and melody rich as an angel's song.

Earth's joy is small, her mirth is trivial, but heaven has sent us joy immeasurable, fit for immortal minds.[21]

---

[21] Joy born at Bethlehem - Sermon delivered 24th December 1871

Day 12 - Never Too Much Joy

And the angel said to them, "Fear not, for behold, I bring you good news of great joy that will be for all the people.
(Luke 2:10 ESV)

The joy of sin is a fire-fountain, having its source in the burning soil of hell, maddening and consuming those who drink its fire-water; of such delights we desire not to drink. To be happy in sin is worse than to be damned, since it is the beginning of grace to feel wretched in sin. God save us from unholy peace and from unholy joy! The joy announced by the angel of the nativity is as pure as it is lasting, as holy as it is great. Let us then always believe concerning the Christian religion that it has its joy within itself.

Let our joy be living water from those sacred wells which the Lord himself has dug. May his joy abide in us, that our joy may be full. Of Christ's joy we cannot have too much, there is no fear of running to excess when his love is the wine we drink. Oh to be plunged in this pure stream of spiritual delights!

And what joy there is in this, for suppose an angel had been our Saviour. He would not have been able to bear the load of my sin or yours. If anything less than God had been set up as the ground of our salvation, it might have been found too frail a foundation. But if he who undertakes to save is none other than the Infinite and the Almighty, then the load of our guilt can be carried upon such shoulders, the stupendous labor of our salvation can be achieved by such a worker, and that with ease: for all things are possible with God, and he is able to save all that come to God by him.

Look! Here is the subject of your joy. The God who made you, and against whom you have offended, has come down from heaven and taken upon himself your nature that he might save you. He has come in the fullness of his glory and the infinity of his mercy that he might redeem you. Do you not welcome this news? What! will not your hearts be thankful for this? Does this matchless love awaken no gratitude? Were it not for this divine Saviour, your life here would have been wretched, and your future existence would have been endless woe.

Oh, I pray you adore the incarnate God, and trust in him. Then you will bless the Lord for delivering you from the wrath to come, and as you lay hold of Jesus and find salvation in his name, you will tune your songs to his praise, and exult with sacred joy. [22]

---

[22] Joy born at Bethlehem - Sermon delivered 24th December 1871

Day 13 - The Sign of True Joy

And this will be a sign for you: you will find a baby wrapped in swaddling cloths and lying in a manger.
(Luke 2:12 ESV)

The sign that the joy of the world had come was this - they were to go to the manger to find the Christ in it, and he was to be the sign. Every circumstance is therefore instructive. The babe was found "wrapped in swaddling clothes." Now, observe, as you look at this infant, that there is not the remotest appearance of temporal power here. Mark the two little puny arms of a little babe that must be carried if it go. Alas, the nations of the earth look for joy in military power. Is it not a nation's pride to be gigantic in arms? What pride flushes the patriot's cheek when he remembers that his nation can murder faster than any other people.

Ah, foolish generation, you are groping in the flames of hell to find your heaven, raking amid blood and bones for the foul thing which you call glory. A nation's joy can never lie in the misery of others. Killing is not the path to prosperity; huge armaments are a curse to the nation itself as well as to its neighbors. The joy of a nation is a golden sand over which no stream of blood has ever rippled. It is only found in that river, the streams whereof make glad the city of God. The weakness of submissive gentleness is true power. Jesus founds his eternal empire not on force but on love. Here, O people, see your hope; the mild peaceful prince, whose glory is his self-sacrifice. He is our true benefactor.

Neither was wealth to be seen at Bethlehem. Here in this quiet island, the bulk of men are comfortably seeking to acquire their thousands by commerce and manufactures. But, here, in the cradle of the world's hope at Bethlehem, I see far more poverty than wealth. I perceive no glitter of gold, or spangle of silver. I perceive only a poor babe, so poor, so very poor, that he is in a manger laid; and his mother is a mechanic's wife. A woman who wears neither silk nor gem.

Not in your gold, will your joy ever lie, but in the gospel enjoyed by all classes, the gospel freely preached and joyfully received. Jesus, by raising us to spiritual wealth, redeems us from the chains of Mammon, and in that liberty gives us joy.[23]

---

[23] Joy born at Bethlehem - Sermon delivered 24th December 1871

Day 14 - Sing For Joy

And the angel said to them, "Fear not, for behold, I bring you good news of great joy that will be for all the people.
(Luke 2:10 ESV)

There are some sombre religionists who were born in a dark night in December that think a smile upon the face is wicked, and believe that for a Christian to be glad and rejoice is to be inconsistent. Ah! I wish these gentlemen had seen the angels when they sang about Christ For if angels sang about his birth, certainly men ought to sing about it as long as they live, sing about it when they die, and sing about it when they live in heaven for ever.

I do long to see in the midst of the church more of a singing Christianity. The last few years have been breeding in our midst a groaning and unbelieving Christianity. Now, I doubt not its sincerity, but I do doubt its healthy character. I say it may be true and real enough. God forbid I should say a word against the sincerity of those who practice it, but it is a sickly religion. Watts hit the mark when he said,

"Religion never was designed

To make our pleasures less."[24]

It is designed to do away with some of our pleasures, but it gives us many more, to make up for what it takes away; so it does not make them less. O, you that see in Christ nothing but a subject to stimulate your doubts and make the tears run down your cheeks. O, you that always say,

"Lord, what a wretched land is this,

That yields us no supplies"[25]

Rejoice in the Lord always, and again I say unto you rejoice[26]. Especially this week do not be

---

[24] We're marching to Zion, Isaac Watts

[25] Lord what a wretched land is this, Isaac Watts

[26] Philippians 4:4

ashamed to be glad. You need not think it is a wicked thing to be happy. Penance and whipping and misery are not such very virtuous things, after all. The damned are miserable; let the saved be happy. Why should you hold fellowship with the lost by feelings of perpetual mourning? Why not rather anticipate the joys of heaven, and begin to sing on earth that song which you will never need to end?

The first emotion that we ought to cherish in our hearts is the emotion of joy and gladness.[27]

---

[27] Joy born at Bethlehem - Sermon delivered 24th December 1871

Day 15 - Glory In The Highest

*And suddenly there was with the angel a multitude of the heavenly host praising God and saying, "**Glory to God in the highest**, and on earth peace among those with whom he is pleased!"*
(Luke 2:13-14 ESV)

What is the instructive lesson to be learned from this first syllable of the angels' song? This - that salvation is God's highest glory.

He is glorified in every dew drop that twinkles to the morning sun. He is magnified in every wood flower that blossoms in the copse, although it live to blush unseen, and waste its sweetness in the forest air. God is glorified in every bird that warbles on the spray; in every lamb that skips the mead. Do not the fishes in the sea praise him? From the tiny minnow to the huge Leviathan, do not all creatures that swim the water bless and praise his name? Do not all created things extol him? Is there anything beneath the sky, save man, that does not glorify God?

Do not the stars exalt him, when they write his name upon the azure of heaven in their golden letters? Do not the lightnings adore him when they flash his brightness in arrows of light piercing the midnight darkness? Do not thunders extol him when they roll like drums in the march of the God of armies? Do not all things exalt him, from the least even to the greatest? But sing, sing, oh universe, till you have exhausted yourself, you can not afford a song so sweet as the song of Incarnation. Though creation may be a majestic organ of praise, it cannot reach the compass of the golden canticle - Incarnation!

Lo! What wisdom is here. God becomes man that God may be just, and the justifier of the ungodly.

Lo! what power, for where is power so great as when it conceals its power? What power, that Godhead should unrobe itself and become man!

Behold, what love is revealed to us when Jesus becomes a man.

Behold, what faithfulness! How many promises are this day kept? How many solemn obligations are this hour discharged?

Tell me one attribute of God that is not manifest in Jesus; and your ignorance shall be the reason why you have not seen it so. The whole of God is glorified in Christ; and though some part of the name of God is written in the universe, it is here best read - in Him who was the Son of Man, and, yet, the Son of God.[28]

[28] Joy born at Bethlehem - Sermon delivered 24th December 1871

Day 16 - Goodwill Towards You

*And suddenly there was with the angel a multitude of the heavenly host praising God and saying, "Glory to God in the highest, and on earth **peace among those with whom he is pleased!"***
(Luke 2:13-14 ESV)

There had been no peace on earth since Adam fell. But, now, when the newborn King made his appearance, the swaddling band with which he was wrapped up was the white flag of peace. That manger was the place where the treaty was signed, whereby warfare should be stopped between man's conscience and himself, man's conscience and his God.

Where else can peace be found, but in the message of Jesus?

Go legalist, work for peace with toil and pain, and you shall never find it. Go, you that trust in the law: go to Sinai; look to the flames that Moses saw, and shrink, and tremble, and despair; for peace is nowhere to be found but in him of whom it is said, "This man shall be peace."[29] And what a peace it is, beloved! It is peace like a river, and righteousness like the waves of the sea. It is the peace of God that surpasses all understanding, which keeps our hearts and minds through Jesus Christ our Lord. This sacred peace between the pardoned soul and God the pardoner; this marvelous at-one-ment between the sinner and his judge, this was it that the angels sung when they said, "peace on earth."

No greater proof of kindness between the Creator and his subjects can possibly be found than when the Creator gives his only begotten and beloved Son to die. Some think of God as if he were a morose being who hated all mankind. Some picture him as if he were some abstract subsistence taking no interest in our affairs. Listen, God has "good will toward men." You know what good will means. Well, swearer, you have cursed God but he has not fulfilled his curse on you. He has good will towards you

---

[29] Micah 5:5

although you have no good will towards him. You have sinned high and hard against the Most High but he has said no hard things against you, for he has good will towards men.

Poor sinner, you have broken his laws, you are half afraid to come to the throne of his mercy in case he should spurn you. Hear this, and be comforted - God has good will towards men, so good a will that he has said, and said it with an oath too, "As I live, declares the Lord GOD, I have no pleasure in the death of the wicked, but that the wicked turn from his way and live"[30]. He has so good a will that he has even said, ""Come now, let us reason together, says the LORD: though your sins are like scarlet, they shall be as white as snow; though they are red like crimson, they shall become like wool."[31]

And if you say, "Lord, how shall I know that you have this good will towards me," he points to the manger, and says, "Sinner, if I had not a good will towards you, would I have parted with my Son? If I had not good will towards the

---

[30] Ezekiel 33:11

[31] Isaiah 1:18

human race, would I have given up my Son to become one of that race that he might by so doing redeem them from death?" You that doubt the Master's love, look to that circle of angels; see their blaze of glory; hear their son, and let your doubts die away in that sweet music and be buried in a shroud of harmony.[32]

[32] Joy born at Bethlehem - Sermon delivered 24th December 1871

Day 17 - Star Preaching

Now after Jesus was born in Bethlehem of Judea in the days of Herod the king, behold, wise men from the east came to Jerusalem, saying, "Where is he who has been born king of the Jews? For we saw his star when it rose and have come to worship him."
(Matthew 2:1-2 ESV)

If it should ever be that men should fail to preach the gospel, God can conduct souls to his Son by a star. Ah! Not only by a star, but by a stone, a bird, a blade of grass, a drop of dew.

Remember that Omnipotence has servants everywhere.

Therefore, do not despair when you hear that one minister has ceased to preach the gospel, or that another is fighting against the truth of God. Their apostasy shall be to their own loss rather than to the hurt of Jesus and his church. And, sad though it is to see the lamps of the sanctuary put out, God is not dependent upon human lights, he is the light of his own holy place. Mortal tongues, if they refuse to preach his word, shall have their places supplied by books in the running brooks and sermons in stones. The beam shall cry out of the wall, and the timber shall answer it.

When chief priests and scribes have all gone out of the way, the Lord puts stars into commission, and once more in very deed the heavens are telling the glory of God, and the firmament is showing his handiwork[33]. Sooner than lack speakers for the incarnate God, mountains and hills shall learn eloquence and break forth into testimony.

God's message shall be made known to the utmost ends of the earth. God shall save his own people. His counsel shall stand, and he will do all his pleasure. Hallelujah!

The star-preaching is all about Christ. We do not know what the color of the star was, nor the shape of the star, nor to what magnitude it had attained; these items are not recorded, but

---

[33] Psalm 19:1

what is recorded is of much more importance; the wise men said—"We have seen *his* star." Then the star which the Lord will use to lead men to Jesus must be Christ's own star. The faithful minister, like this star, belongs to Christ; he is Christ's own man in the most emphatic sense.

Every beam in that star shone forth for Jesus. It was his star, always, and only, and altogether. It shone not for itself, but only as his star.[34]

---

[34] The star and the wise men - Sermon delivered 24th December 1882

Day 18 - Wise Men

Now after Jesus was born in Bethlehem of Judea in the days of Herod the king, behold, wise men from the east came to Jerusalem, saying, "Where is he who has been born king of the Jews? For we saw his star when it rose and have come to worship him."

After listening to the king, they went on their way. And behold, the star that they had seen when it rose went before them until it came to rest over the place where the child was. When they saw the star, they rejoiced exceedingly with great joy. And going into the house, they saw the child with Mary his mother, and they fell down and worshiped him. Then, opening their treasures, they offered him gifts, gold and frankincense and myrrh.
(Matthew 2:1-2, 9-11 ESV)

The wise men did not content themselves with admiring the star and comparing it with other stars, and taking notes as to the exact date of its appearance, and how many times it twinkled, and when it moved, and all that; but they practically used the teaching of the star.

Many are hearers and admirers of God's servants, but they are not wise enough to make fit and proper use of the preaching. They notice the peculiarity of the preacher's language, whether he coughs too often, or speaks too much in his throat; whether he is too loud or too low; whether he has a provincial tone, whether there may be about him a commonness of speech approaching to vulgarity; or, on the other hand, whether he may be too flowery in his diction. Such fooleries as these are the constant observations of men for whose souls we labor. They are perishing, and yet toying with such small matters.

Such is the sport of fools; but these were wise men, and therefore practical men. They did not become star-gazers, and stop at the point of admiring the remarkable star; but they said, "Where is he that is born King of the Jews? for we have seen his star in the east, and are come to worship him." They set out at once to find the now-born King, of whose coming the star was the signal. Oh, my dear hearers, how I wish that you were all wise in this same manner! I would sooner preach the dullest sermon that was ever preached than preach the most brilliant that was ever spoken if I could by that poor sermon lead you quite away from myself to seek the Lord Jesus Christ.

That is the one thing I care about. Will you never gratify me by enquiring after my Lord and Master? I long to hear you say, "What is the man talking about? He speaks about a Savior; we will have that Savior for ourselves. He talks about pardon through the blood of Christ; he speaks about God coming down among men to save them; we will find out if there is any reality in this pardon, any truth in this salvation. We will seek Jesus, and find for ourselves the blessings which are reported to be laid up in him." If I heard you all saying this I should be ready to die of joy.

These men were wise - and I commend their example to you - because when they saw the child they worshipped. Theirs was not curiosity gratified, but devotion exercised.

Enter the house and worship! Forget the preacher. Let the starlight shine for other eyes. Jesus was born that you might be born again.

He lived that you might live. He died that you might die to sin. He is risen, and today he makes intercession for transgressors that they may be reconciled to God through him. Come, then; believe, trust, rejoice, adore! If you have neither gold, frankincense, nor myrrh, bring your faith, your love, your repentance and, falling down before the Son of God, pay him the reverence of your hearts.[35]

---

[35] The star and the wise men - Sermon delivered 24th December 1882

Day 19 - The Days Of Fear Are Over

And in the same region there were shepherds
out in the field, keeping watch over their flock
by night. And an angel of the Lord appeared to
them, and the glory of the Lord shone around
them, and they were filled with great fear. And
the angel said to them, "Fear not, for behold, I
bring you good news of great joy that will be for
all the people.
(Luke 2:8-10 ESV)

No sooner did the angel of the Lord appear to the shepherds, and the glory of the Lord shine round about them, than they were afraid. It had come to this, that man was afraid of his God, and when God sent down his loving messengers with tidings of great joy, men were filled with as much fright as though the angel of death had appeared with uplifted sword.

The silence of night and it's dreary gloom caused no fear in the shepherds' hearts, but the joyful herald of the skies, robed in glories of grace, made them afraid. We must not condemn the shepherds on this account as though they were peculiarly timid or ignorant, for they were only acting as every other person in that age would have done under the same circumstances. Not because they were simple shepherds were they amazed with fear, but it is probable that if they had been well-instructed prophets they would have displayed the same feeling; for there are many instances recorded in Scripture, in which the foremost men of their time trembled and felt a horror of great darkness when special manifestations of God were shown to them.

When he heard the voice of the Lord God walking in the garden in the cool of the day, Adam was afraid and hid himself from the presence of the Lord God amongst the trees of the garden.[36] Sin makes miserable cowards of us all. See the man who once could hold delightful conversations with his Maker, now dreading to hear his Maker's voice and skulking in the grove like a felon, who knows his guilt, and is afraid to meet the officers of justice.

---

[36] Genesis 3:8-10

Beloved, in order to remove this nightmare of slavish fear from the breast of humanity, where it's horrible influence represses all the noblest aspirations of the soul, our Lord Jesus Christ came in the flesh. This is one of the works of the devil which he was manifested to destroy. Angels came to proclaim the good news of the advent of the incarnate God, and the very first note of their song was a foretaste of the sweet result of his coming to all those who shall receive him.

The angel said, "Fear not," as though the times of fear were over, and the days of hope and joy had arrived. "Fear not." These words were not meant for those trembling shepherds only, but were intended for you and for me, and all nations to whom the glad tidings shall come. " Fear not." Let God no longer be the object of your slavish dread! Stand not at a distance from him any more. The Word is made flesh. God has descended to tabernacle among men, that there may be no hedge of fire, no yawning gulf between God and man.[37]

---

[37] God incarnate, the end of fear - Sermon delivered 23rd December 1866

Day 20 - The Remedy To Fear

And in the same region there were shepherds out in the field, keeping watch over their flock by night. And an angel of the Lord appeared to them, and the glory of the Lord shone around them, and they were filled with great fear. And the angel said to them, "Fear not, for behold, I bring you good news of great joy that will be for all the people. For unto you is born this day in the city of David a Savior, who is Christ the Lord. And this will be a sign for you: you will find a baby wrapped in swaddling cloths and lying in a manger."
(Luke 2:8-12 ESV)

This is the remedy to fear: God with us. God made flesh.

According to the text the shepherds were not to fear, because the angel had come to bring them good news. How does it run? It says, "I bring you good news of great joy." But what was this gospel? Further on we are told that the gospel was the fact that Christ was born. So, then, it is good news to men that Christ is born, that God has come down and taken manhood into union with himself.

Indeed this is good news. He who made the heavens slumbers in a manger. What does this mean? That God is not of necessity an enemy to man, because here is God actually taking manhood into alliance with Deity.

The Eternal seems to be so far away from us. He is infinite, and we are such little creatures. There appears to be a great gulf fixed between man and God, even on the ground of creatureship. But observe, he who is God has also become man. We never heard that God took the nature of angels into union with himself; we may therefore say that between Godhead and angel-hood there must be an infinite distance still; but here the Lord has actually taken manhood into union with himself; there is therefore no longer a great gulf fixed, on the contrary, here is a marvellous union; Godhead has entered into marriage bonds with manhood.

O my soul, you do not stand now like a poor lone orphan wailing across the deep sea after your Father who has gone far away and cannot hear you. You do not now sob and sigh like an infant left naked and helpless, its Maker having gone too far away to regard its wants or listen to its cries. No, your Maker has become like you. Is that too strong a word to use? He without whom nothing was made that was made is that same Word who tabernacled among us and was made flesh, made flesh in such a way that he was tempted in all points like as we are, yet without sin.

O manhood, was there ever such news as this for you! Poor manhood, you weak worm of the dust, far lower than the angels, lift up your head, and be not afraid! Poor manhood, born in weakness, living in toil, covered with sweat, and dying at last to be eaten by the worms, do not be ashamed even in the presence of angels, for next to God is man, and not even an archangel can come in between.

Jesus Christ, eternally God, was born, and lived and died as we also do. That is the first word of comfort to expel our fear.[38]

Day 21 - Born For This

And the angel said to them, "Fear not, for behold, I bring you good news of great joy that will be for all the people. For unto you is born this day in the city of David a Savior, who is Christ the Lord. And this will be a sign for you: you will find a baby wrapped in swaddling cloths and lying in a manger."
(Luke 2:10-12 ESV)

Our Lord Jesus Christ is in some senses more man than Adam. Adam was not born; Adam never had to struggle through the risks and weaknesses of infancy. He knew not the littlenesses of childhood - he was full grown at once. Father Adam could not sympathize with me as a babe and a child. But how man-like is Jesus! he is cradled with us in the manger; he does not begin with us in mid-life, as Adam, but he accompanies us in the pains and feebleness and infirmities of infancy, and he continues with us even to the grave.

Beloved, this is such sweet comfort. He that is God this day was once an infant so that if my cares are little and even trivial and comparatively infantile, I may go to him, for he was once a child. Though the great ones of the earth may sneer at the child of poverty, and say, "You are too insignificant, and your trouble is too slight for pity;" I recollect with humble joy, that the King of heaven did hang upon a woman's breast, and was wrapped in swaddling bands, and therefore I tell him all my griefs.

How wonderful that he should have been an infant, and yet should be God over all, blessed for ever! I am not afraid of God now; this blessed link between me and God, the holy child Jesus, has taken all fear away.

Observe, the angel told them somewhat of his office, as well as of his birth. "Unto you is born this day a Saviour." The very object for which he was born and came into this world was that he might deliver us from sin. What, then, was it that made us afraid? Were we not afraid of God because we felt that we were lost through sin? Well then, here is joy upon joy. Here is not only the Lord come among us as a man, but made man in order to save man from that which separated him from God.

I feel as if I could burst out into a weeping for some here who have been spending their living riotously and gone far away from God their Father by their evil ways. I know they are afraid to come back. They think that the Lord will not receive them, that there is no mercy for such sinners as they have been. Oh, but think of it — Jesus Christ has come to seek and to save that which was lost. He was born to save. If he does not save he was born in vain, for the object of his birth was salvation. If he shall not be a Saviour, then the mission of God to earth has missed its end, for its design was that lost sinners might be saved.

God has come; the Infinite, the Almighty, has stooped from the highest heaven that he may pick you up, a poor undone and worthless worm. Is there not comfort here? Does not the incarnate Saviour take away the horrible dread which hangs over men like a black cloud?[39]

---

[39] God incarnate, the end of fear - Sermon delivered 23rd December 1866

Day 22 - Fear Not

And the angel said to them, "Fear not, for behold, I bring you good news of great joy that will be for all the people. For unto you is born this day in the city of David a Savior, who is Christ the Lord. And this will be a sign for you: you will find a baby wrapped in swaddling cloths and lying in a manger." And suddenly there was with the angel a multitude of the heavenly host praising God and saying,
"Glory to God in the highest,
and on earth peace among
those with whom he is pleased!"
(Luke 2:10-14 ESV)

Child of God, you say, "I dare not come to God today, I feel so weak." Fear not, for he that is born in Bethlehem said, "A bruised reed I will not break, and the smoking flax I will not quench."[40]

"I shall never get to heaven," says another; "I shall never see God's face with acceptance; I am

---

[40] Isaiah 42:3

so tempted." "Fear not," For you do not have a high priest who is unable to sympathize with our weaknesses, but one who in every respect has been tempted as we are, yet without sin."[41]

"But I am so lonely in the world," says another, "no man cares for me." There is one man at any rate who does so care; a true man like yourself. He is your brother still, and does not forget the lonely spirit.

But I hear a sinner say, "I am afraid to go to God this morning and confess that I am a sinner." Well, do not go to God but go to Christ. Surely you would not be afraid of him. Think of God in Christ, not out of Christ. If you could know Jesus you would go to him at once; you would not be afraid to tell him your sins, for you would know that he would say, "Go, and sin no more."[42]

"I cannot pray," says one, "I feel afraid to pray." What, afraid to pray when it is a man who listens to you? You might dread the face of God,

[41] Hebrews 4:15

[42] John 8:11

but when God in human flesh you see why be alarmed? Go, poor sinner, go to Jesus.

"I feel," says one, "unfit to come." You may be unfit to come to God, but you cannot be unfit to come to Jesus. There is a fitness necessary to stand in the holy hill of the Lord, but there is no fitness needed in coming to the Lord Jesus. Come as you are, guilty, and lost, and ruined. Come just as you are, and he will receive you.

"Oh," says another, "I cannot trust." I can understand your not being able to trust the great invisible God, but cannot you trust that dying, bleeding Son of Man who is also the Son of God?

"But I cannot hope," says another, "that he would even look on me:" Yet he used to look on those like you. He received publicans and sinners and ate with them, and even harlots were not driven from his presence. Oh, since God has taken man into union with himself be not afraid! If I speak to one who by reason of sin has wandered so far away from God that he is even afraid to think of God's name, Jesus Christ is called "the sinner's Friend," I pray you think of him, poor soul, as your friend. And, oh! may the Spirit of God open your blind eyes to see that there is no cause for you keeping away from God, except your own mistaken thoughts of him! May you believe that he is able and willing to save to the uttermost! May you understand his good and gracious character, his readiness to pass by transgression, iniquity, and sin! And may the sweet influences of grace constrain you to come to him this very morning!

May God grant that Jesus Christ may be formed in you, the hope of glory; and then you may well sing, "Glory to God in the highest; on earth peace, and goodwill toward men." Amen.[43]

---

[43] God incarnate, the end of fear - Sermon delivered 23rd December 1866

Day 23 - Full Of Grace And Truth

And the Word became flesh and dwelt among us, and we have seen his glory, glory as of the only Son from the Father, full of grace and truth.
(John 1:14 ESV)

Now, you remember that in the Jewish Church its greatest glory was that God tabernacled in its midst: not the tent of Moses, not the various pavilions of the princes of the twelve tribes, but the humble tabernacle in which God dwelt, was the boast of Israel. They had the king himself in the midst of them, a present God in their midst.

The tabernacle was a tent to which men went when they would commune with God, and it was the spot to which God came when he would commune with man. Here they met each other through the slaughter of the bullock and the lamb, and there was reconciliation between them.

Now, Christ's human flesh was God's tabernacle, and it is in Christ that God meets with man, and in Christ that man has dealings with God. The Jew of old went to God's tent, in the center of the camp, if he would worship: we come to Christ if we would pay our homage. If the Jew would be released from ceremonial uncleanness, after he had performed the rites, he went up to the sanctuary of his God, that he might feel again that there was peace between God and his soul. We, having been washed in the precious blood of Christ, have access with boldness unto God, even the Father through Christ, who is our tabernacle and the tabernacle of God among men.

The greatest glory of the tabernacle itself was the most holy place. In the most holy place there stood the ark of the covenant, bearing its golden lid called the mercy-seat. Over the mercy-seat stood the cherubim, whose wings met each other, and beneath the wings of the cherubim there was a bright light, known to the Hebrew believer by the name of the Shekinah. That light represented the presence of God. Immediately above that light there might be seen at night a pillar of fire, and by day a spiral column of cloud rose from it. The glory of the tabernacle was the Shekinah. What does our text say? Jesus Christ was God's tabernacle.

However, there is a surpassing excellence in Christ the tabernacle, by which he wondrously excels that of the Jewish Church. "Full of grace and truth." The Jewish tabernacle was rather full of law than full of grace. It is true there were in its rites and ceremonies, foreshadowings of grace, but still in repeated sacrifice there was renewed remembrance of sin, and a man had first to be obedient to the law of ceremonies, before he could have access to the tabernacle at all. But Christ is full of grace - not a little of it - but abundance of it is treasured up in him.

The tabernacle of old was not full of truth, but full of image, and shadow, and symbol, and picture; but Christ is full of substance. He is not the picture, but the reality; he is not the shadow, but the substance. O believer, rejoice with joy unspeakable for you come to Christ, the real tabernacle of God. You come to him who is full of the glory of the Father; and you come to one in whom you have not the representation of a grace which you needest, but the grace itself - not the shadow of a truth ultimately to be revealed, but that very truth by which your soul is accepted in the sight of God.[44]

[44] The glory of Christ beheld - Sermon delivered 20th October 1861

Day 24 - Behold His Glory

And the Word became flesh and dwelt among us, and we have seen his glory, glory as of the only Son from the Father, full of grace and truth.
(John 1:14 ESV)

"We have seen his glory." It does not say we heard of his glory, we read of it in prophecy, or we listened to it from the lips of others, but we have seen his glory. What a privilege was this, which was accorded to the first disciples! Have you not often envied them? To see the man, the very man, in whom God dwelt. To walk with him as one's companion along his journeys of mercy. To listen to the words as they stream all living from those eloquent lips. To look into his eyes, and mark the depth of love that glistened there. To see his face.

All this is carnal, all this is of sight, and the Christian is a nobler being than to live and walk by sight. He lives by faith; and to this day, there is a sight of Christ which can be had by faith. Therefore, we need not murmur because we are denied the privilege of sight. The sight of

Christ it seems, did little good to those who had it, not even to his disciples. It was only when the Spirit came down at Pentecost, that they began to know Christ, and to understand what he had said to them, though he himself had said it.

Truly it is better to see Christ by faith than it is to see him by sight, for a sight of him by faith saves the soul; but we might see him with the eye, and yet crucify him, yet be found amongst the greatest rebels against his government and power.

Have you beheld his glory by faith? Happy is the man whose lips are ever overflowing with the news of Jesus! Blessed is he whose ministry is full of Christ! He is blessed in his own soul, as well as blessing others. You have heard of it, then, but what of all this? You may hear of his glory and perish in your sins. You have read of his glory; this book is in your houses, and you read it. And you know how he ascended on high, leading captivity captive, and ever sits at the right hand of God. But you may read all this; and yet it shall be a curse and not a blessing, for you knew him and yet rejected him. You were among his own and he came to you, and you received him not. Oh! to behold his glory! This is soul work, saving work, blessed work, everlasting work: have you any interest in it?

But you answer, "How can we see his glory?" Why, faith sees it. Faith looks back to the man who lived and died for us, and sees glory in his shame, honor in his disgraces, riches in his poverty, might in his weakness, triumph in his conflict, and immortality in his death.

Faith is sometimes assisted by experience; and experience sees his glory: it sees the glory of his grace in rolling away all our sins; the preciousness of his blood in giving us reconciliation with the Father; the power of the Spirit in subduing the will; the love of his heart in constantly remembering us upon the throne; and the power of his plea in its perpetual prevalence with God. Experience shows us the glory of Christ in the deep waters, while he puts his arm beneath us and says, "Fear not, thou shalt not be drowned." It shows us the glory in the blazing furnace while the Son of Man treads the glowing coals with his afflicted Israel. Experience shows us the glory of Christ in all the attacks of Satan. While he is our shield he wards off every poisoned arrow, shows us the glory of Christ in helping us to live and enabling us to die, and it shall show us the glory of Christ in enabling us to rise and take possession of the crown which he hath purchased for his children.[45]

---

[45] The glory of Christ beheld - Sermon delivered 20th October 1861

Day 25 - Jesus

Brothers and sisters, instead of preaching let me bear my testimony; my testimony of what I have seen, what my own ears have heard, and my own heart has tasted - that Christ is the only begotten of the Father.

He is divine to me, if he be human to all the world besides. He has done that for me which none but a God could do. He has turned my stubborn will, melted a heart of adamant, broken a chain of steel, opened the gates of brass, and snapped the bars of iron. He has turned for me my mourning into laughter, and my desolation into joy, he has led my captivity captive, made my heart rejoice with joy unspeakable and full of glory. Let others think as they will of him, to me he must be the only begotten of the Father: blessed be his name.

Again, I bear my testimony that he is full of grace. Ah! Had he not been, I should never have beheld his glory. I was full of sin to overflowing. I was condemned already, because I believed not upon him. He drew me when I wanted not to come, and though I struggled hard, he continued still to draw; and when at last I came all trembling like a condemned culprit to his mercy-seat, he said, "Your sins which were many are all forgiven, be of good cheer."

"He drew me up from the pit of destruction, out of the miry bog, and set my feet upon a rock, making my steps secure. He put a new song in my mouth, a song of praise to our God."[46] Let others despise him; but I bear witness that he is full of grace. Oh, remember that Christ is full of grace:

As he is full of grace he is full of truth. True have his promises been, not one has failed. I have often doubted him, for that I blush; he has never failed me, in this I must rejoice. His promises have been yes and amen. I speak the testimony of every believer in Christ, though I put it personally to make it more forcible. I bear witness that never servant had such a Master as I have; never brother had such a kinsman as he has been to me; never spouse had such a husband as Christ has been to my soul; never

---

[46] Psalm 40:1-3

sinner a better Savior; never soldier a better captain; never mourner a better comforter than Christ hath been to my spirit.

I want none beside him. In life he is my life, and in death he shall be the death of death. In poverty Christ is our riches, in sickness he makes our bed. In darkness he is our star, and in brightness he is our sun.[47]

---

[47] The glory of Christ beheld - Sermon delivered 20th October 1861

What Next?

For daily encouragement from Spurgeon's archives, try **spurgeondaily.substack.com**

The Bank of Faith: 365 daily
devotional readings from Charles
Spurgeon

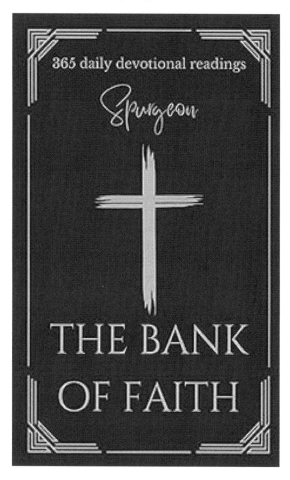

"Oh, that I might comfort some of my Master's servants! I have written out of my own heart with the view of comforting their hearts. I would say to them in their trials -- My brethren, God is good. He will nor forsake you: He will bear you through. There is a promise prepared for your present emergencies; and if you will believe and plead it through Jesus Christ, you shall see the hand of the Lord stretched out to help you. Everything else will fail, but His word never will. He has been to me so faithful in countless instances that I must encourage you to trust Him"

Slow down this year and reflect on the promises of God with this 365-day devotional guide.

All Things New: Daily devotional readings for January from Charles Spurgeon

"Oh, that I might comfort some of my Master's servants! I have written out of my own heart with the view of comforting their hearts. I would say to them in their trials -- My brethren, God is good. He will nor forsake you: He will bear you through. There is a promise prepared for your present emergencies; and if you will believe and plead it through Jesus Christ, you shall see the hand of the Lord stretched out to help you. Everything else will fail, but His word never will. He has been to me so faithful in countless instances that I must encourage you to trust Him"

Slow down this January and reflect on the promises of God with this devotional guide.

The Cross: 40 daily devotional readings on the cross of Christ from Charles Spurgeon

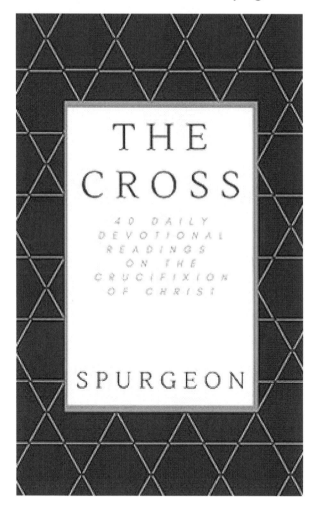

THE
CROSS

40 DAILY
DEVOTIONAL
READINGS
ON THE
CRUCIFIXION
OF CHRIST

SPURGEON

"We have often read the story of our Saviour's sufferings; but we cannot read it too often" said Charles Spurgeon as he opened his Bible to Luke's account of the crucifixion, "Let us, therefore, once again return to the place called Calvary".

Take 10 minutes each day and let Spurgeon warm your heart with joy that can only be found in the good news of Jesus Christ.

The Prince of Preachers examines the atonement with rich imagery and penetrating insight on the journey to Golgotha and Jesus' cries from the cross. Morning or evening, fill your mind with meditation on Jesus' death in your place.

These daily devotional readings have been taken from a selection of Spurgeon's sermons on the cross and the language has been updated for the modern reader

A Child is Born: daily readings for advent
from Charles Spurgeon

These daily devotional readings will warm your heart with the joy that can only be found in the good news of Jesus Christ. Slow down this December and find inspiration in Charles Spurgeon's reflections on the prophecies of Jesus' birth in Isaiah 9.

"This is the season of the year when, whether we wish it or not, we are compelled to think of the birth of Christ." said Charles Spurgeon at the start of his sermon on 23rd December 1855. After dispelling any notion of a religious necessity of celebrating Christmas, he went on, "However, I wish there were ten or a dozen Christmas-days in the year" as an opportunity to preach on the incarnation of Jesus.

Made in the USA
Columbia, SC
03 December 2024

4a379acf-da9a-473f-b94d-a801a074b707R01